Adult Coloring Book

STEAMPUNK STYLE

By L. J. Nance

Adult Coloring Book
Steampunk Style

By L. J. Nance

ISBN-13: 978-1516921706

ISBN-10: 1516921704

Lately, adults are finding that coloring is an excellent way to relieve stress. It takes us back to a happier time in childhood for one thing. Also, it allows people to focus on a task that keeps them from worrying about the stresses in their lives for a space of time. Sort of like meditation...with color.

What better way to let off steam than to immerse yourself in some steampunk designs? If you don't know what steampunk is, think of Jules Verne era tales, or Victorian times when steam was the power of the day. Iconic images of this genre are top hats, airships, octopuses, corsets on the outside, clockwork parts and Tesla-style inventions.

I hope you'll enjoy escaping into an imaginary Victorian universe in this steampunk coloring book. So, grab your colored pens and pencils and dive in. (Feel free to use more colors than brown and black, too.) Let the coloring begin. Huzzah!

Ooo, shiny! Gears and cogs!

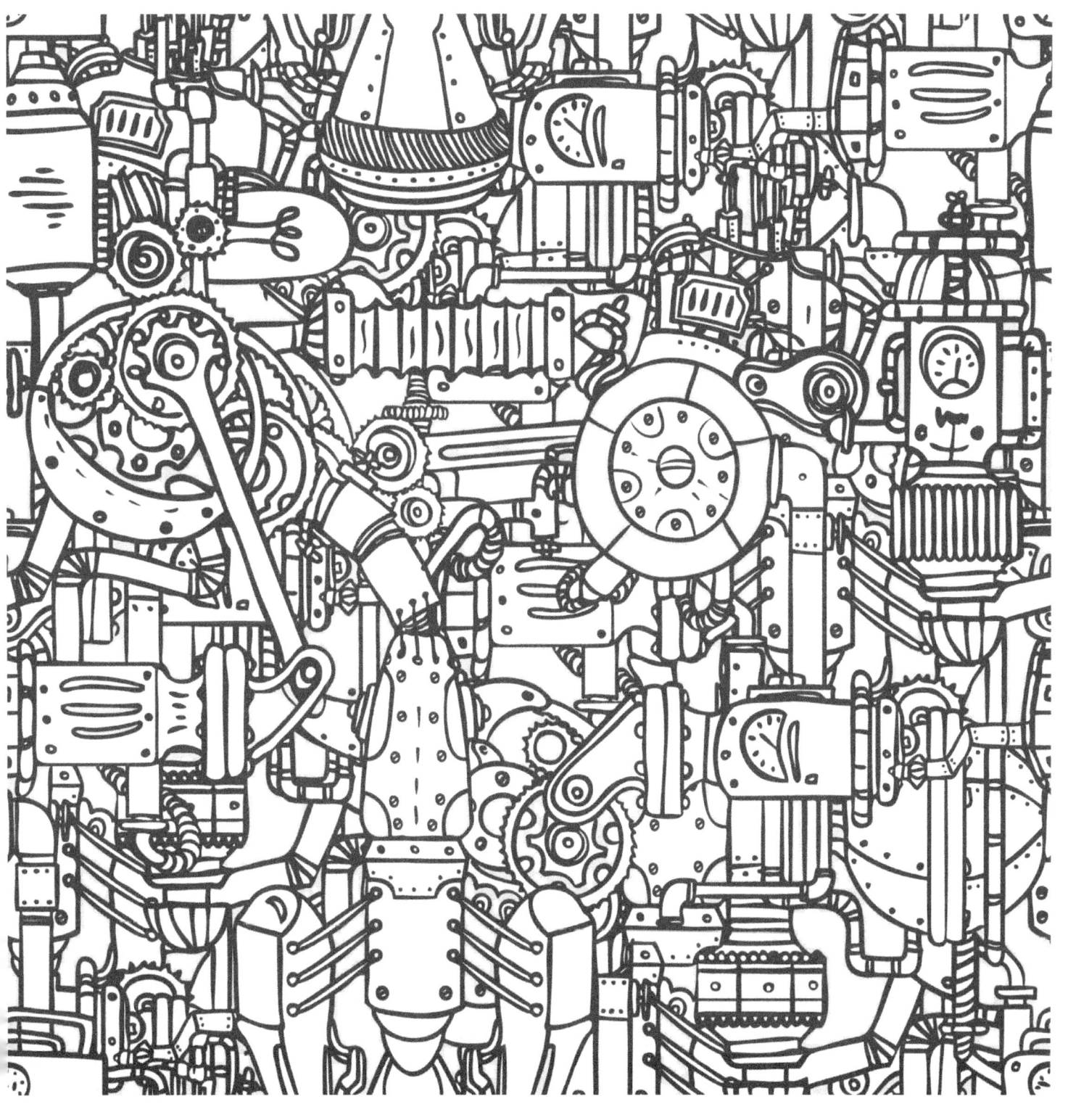

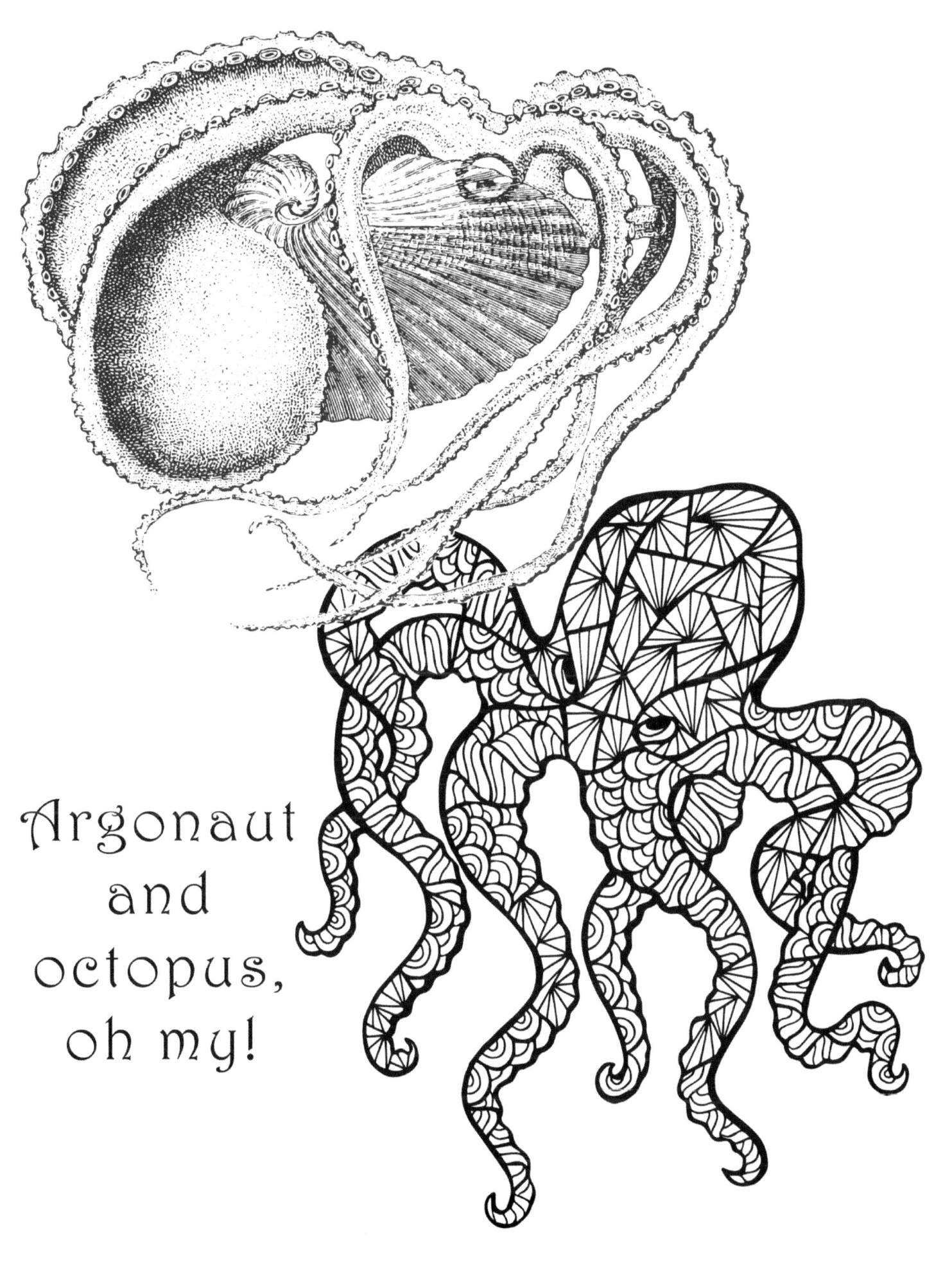

Argonaut
and
octopus,
oh my!

Vintage Victorian Lace

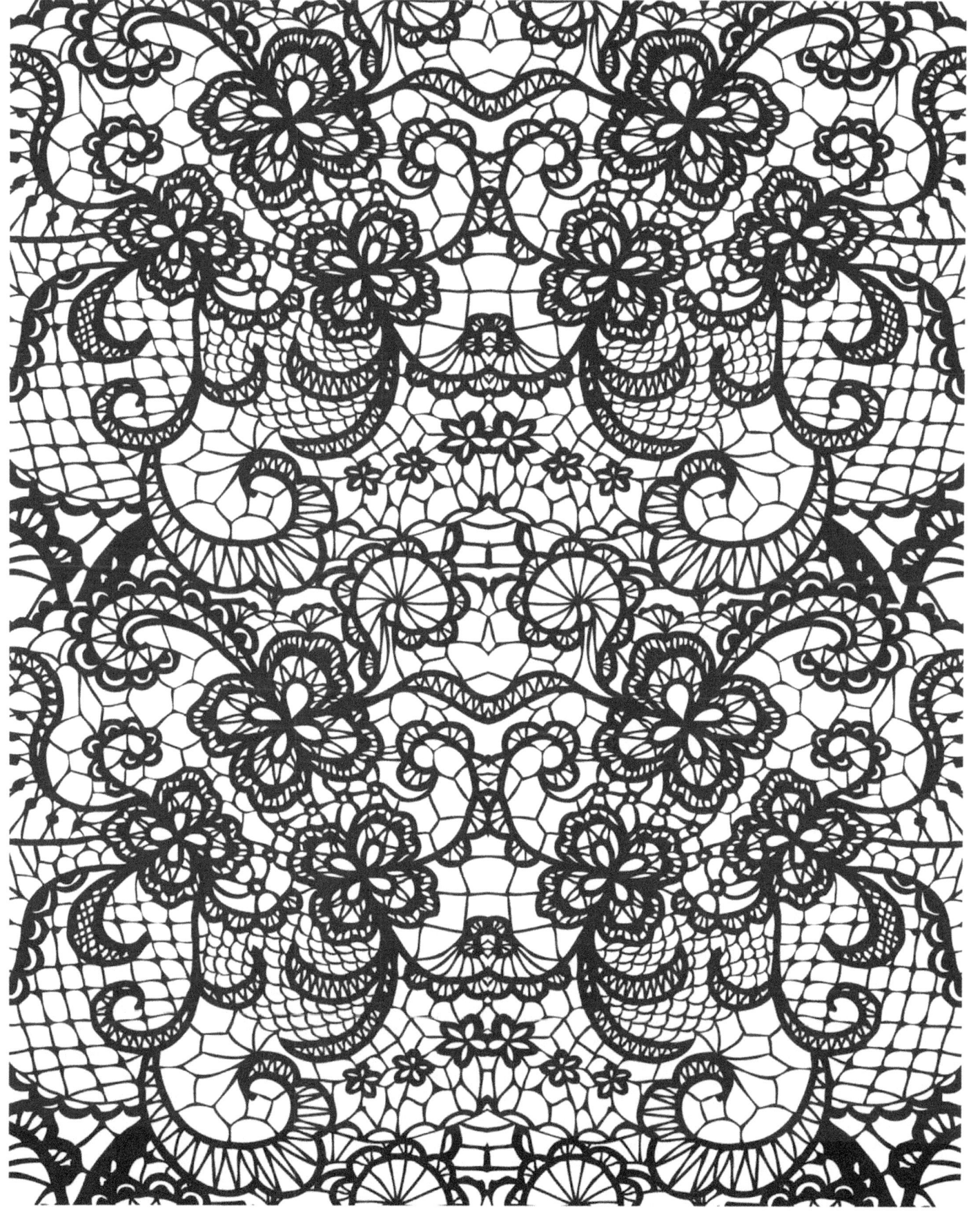

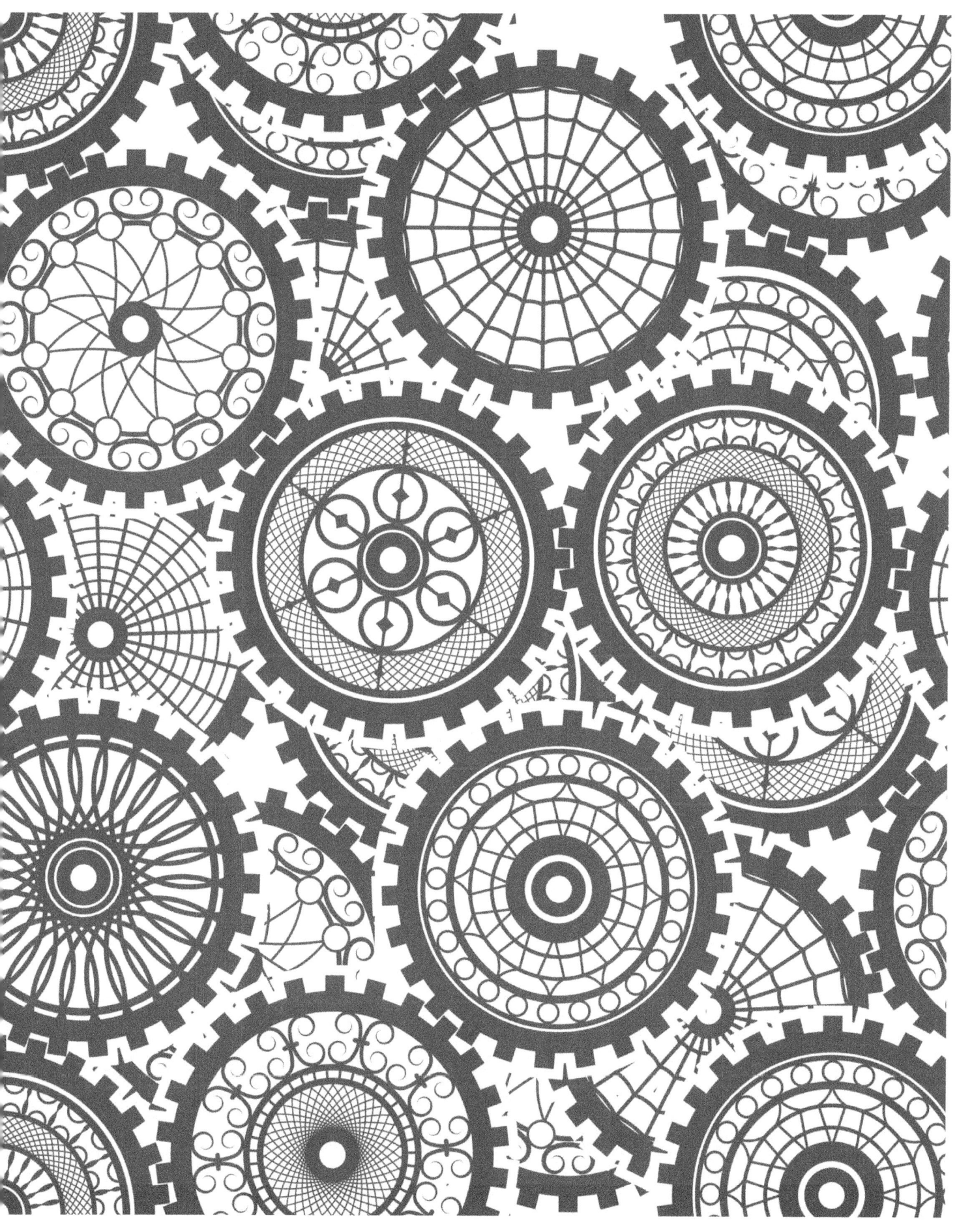

Guide the automaton through the maze!

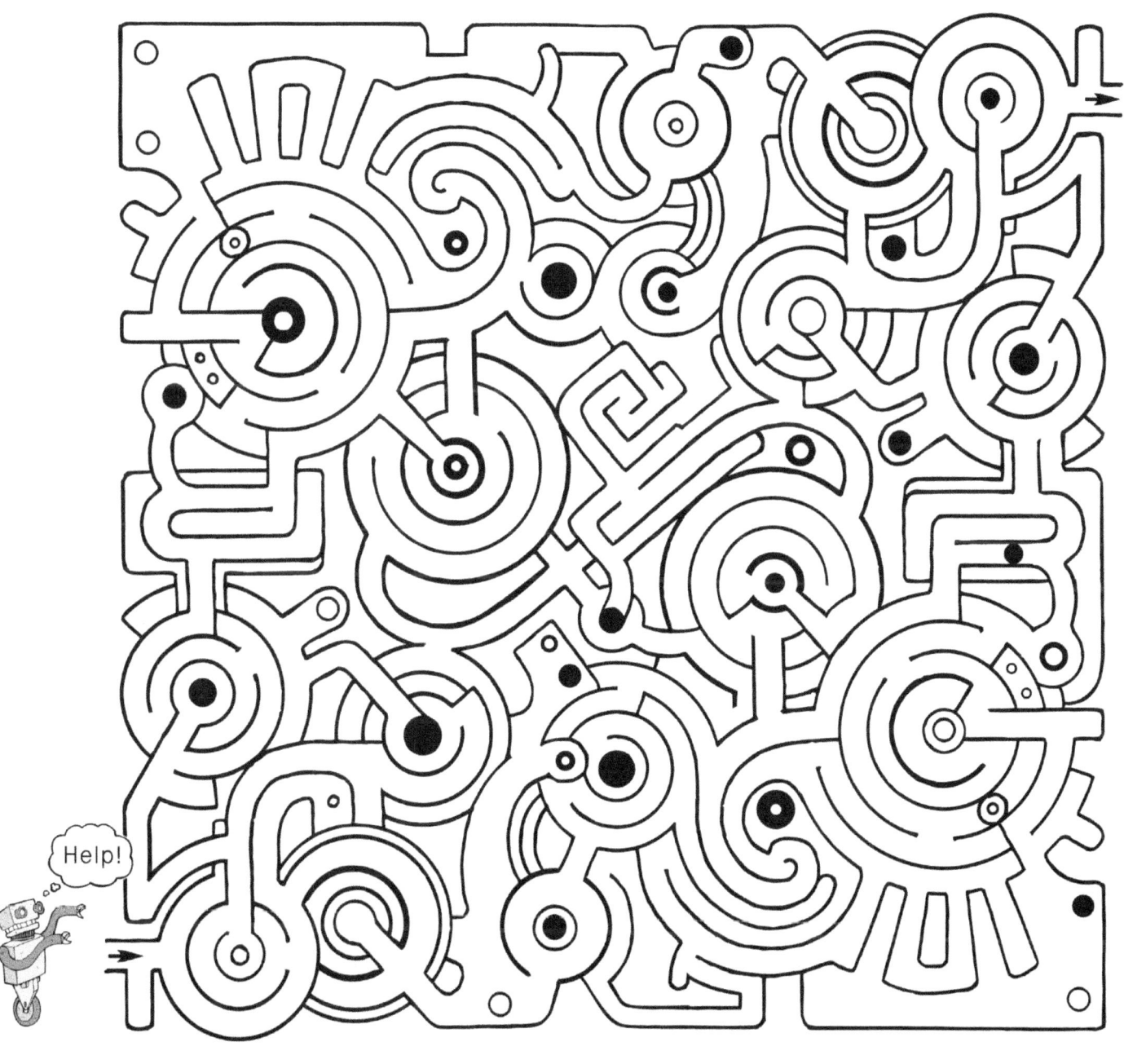

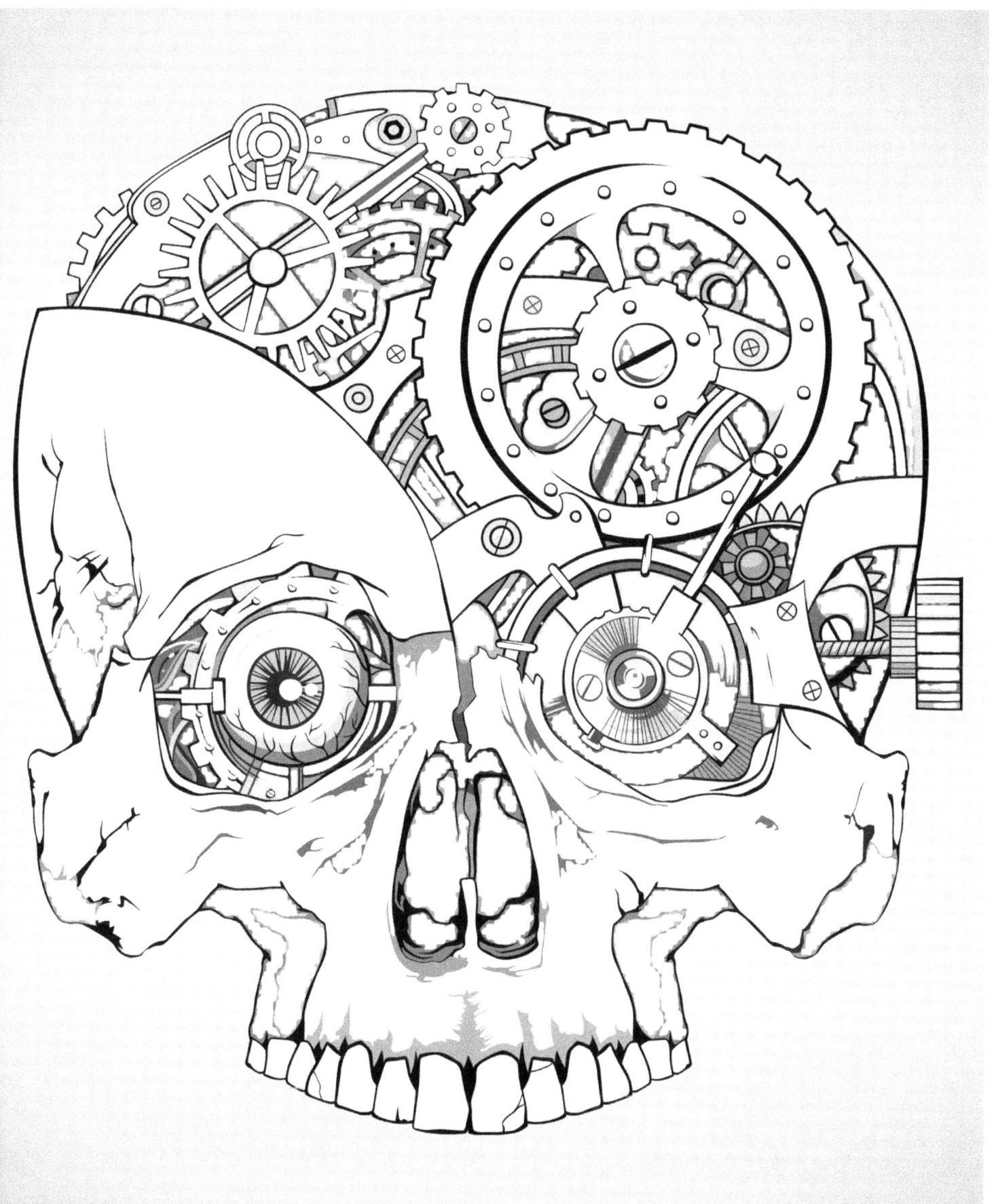

Vintage Victorian Lace II

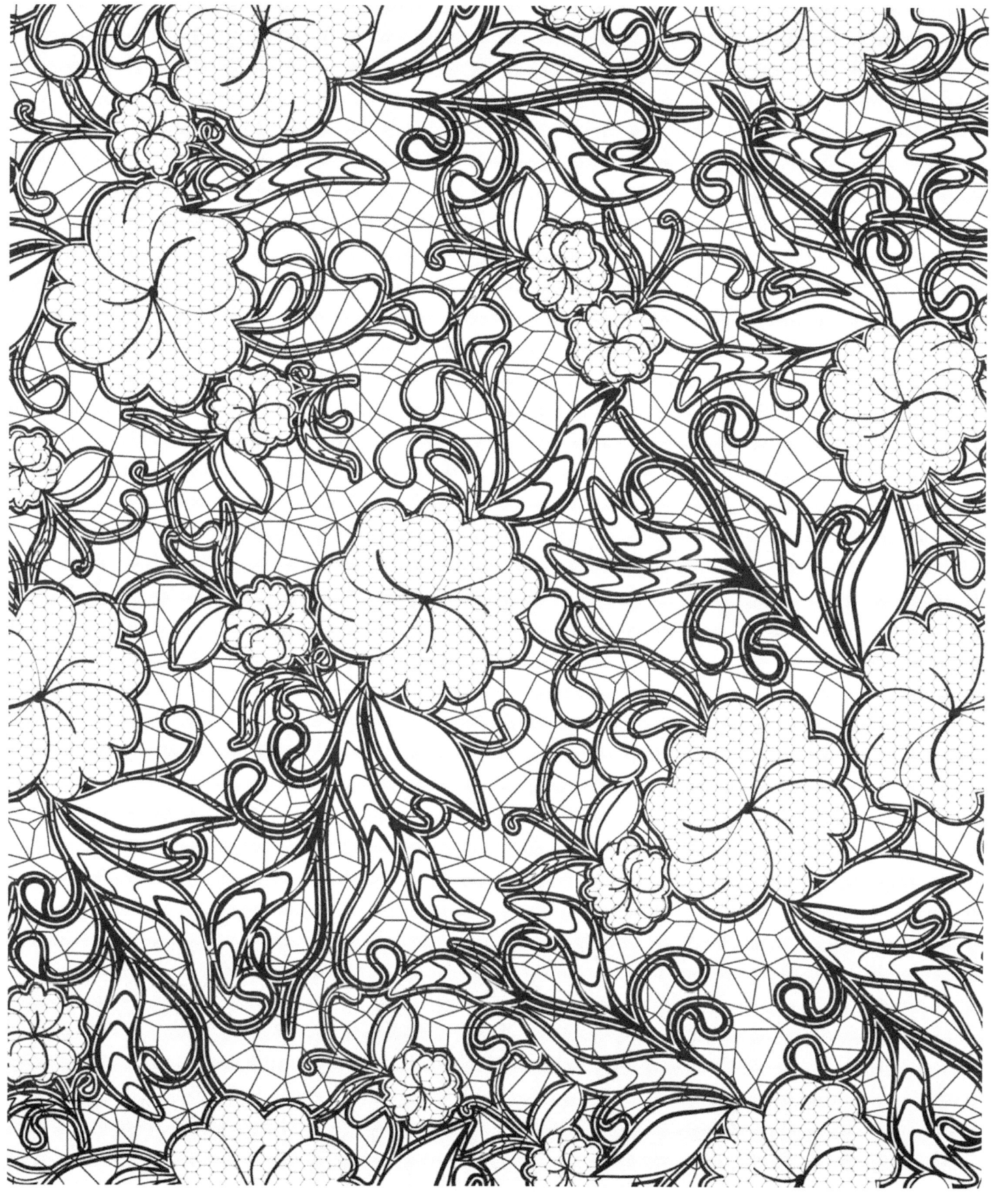

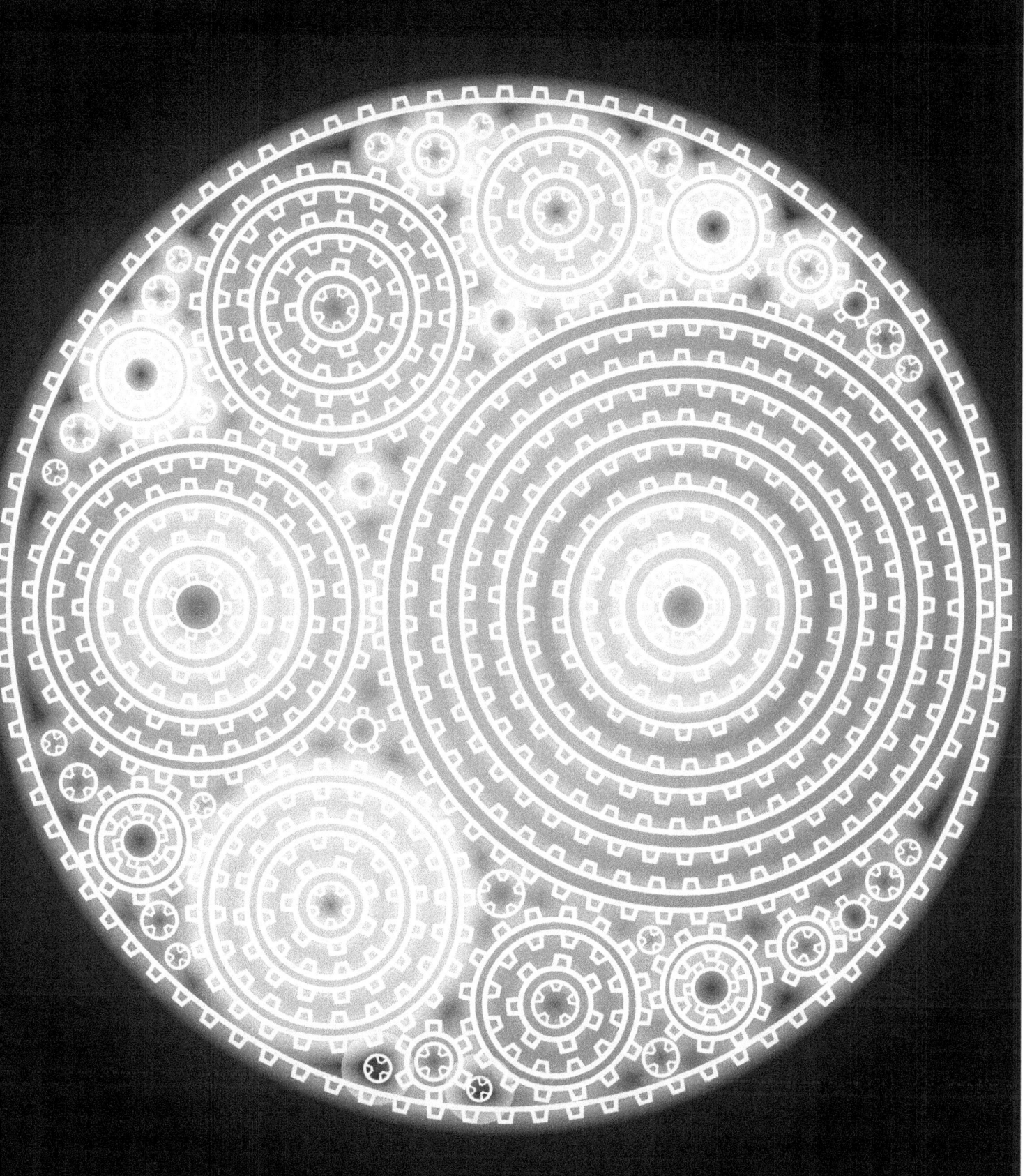

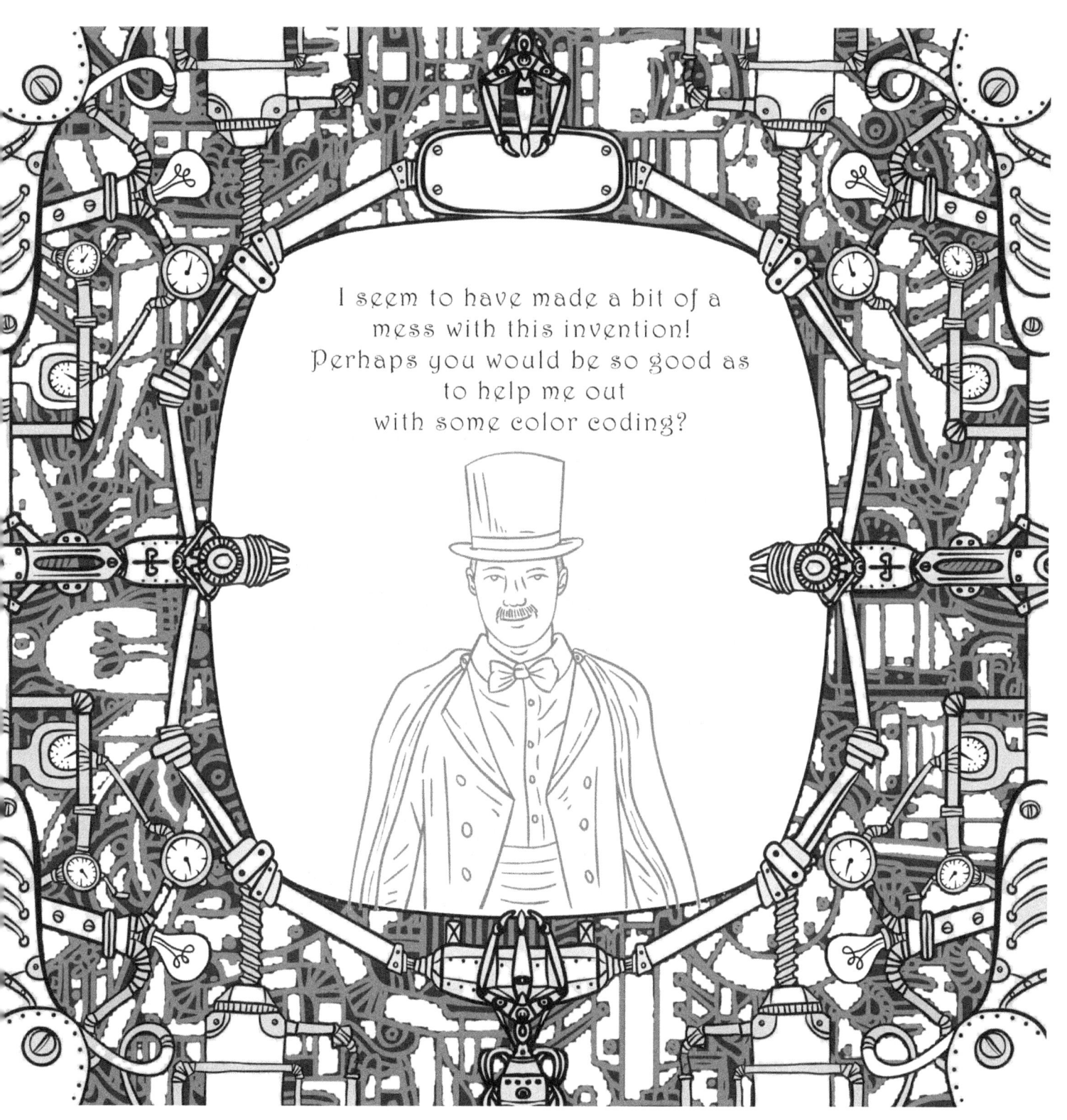

I seem to have made a bit of a
mess with this invention!
Perhaps you would be so good as
to help me out
with some color coding?

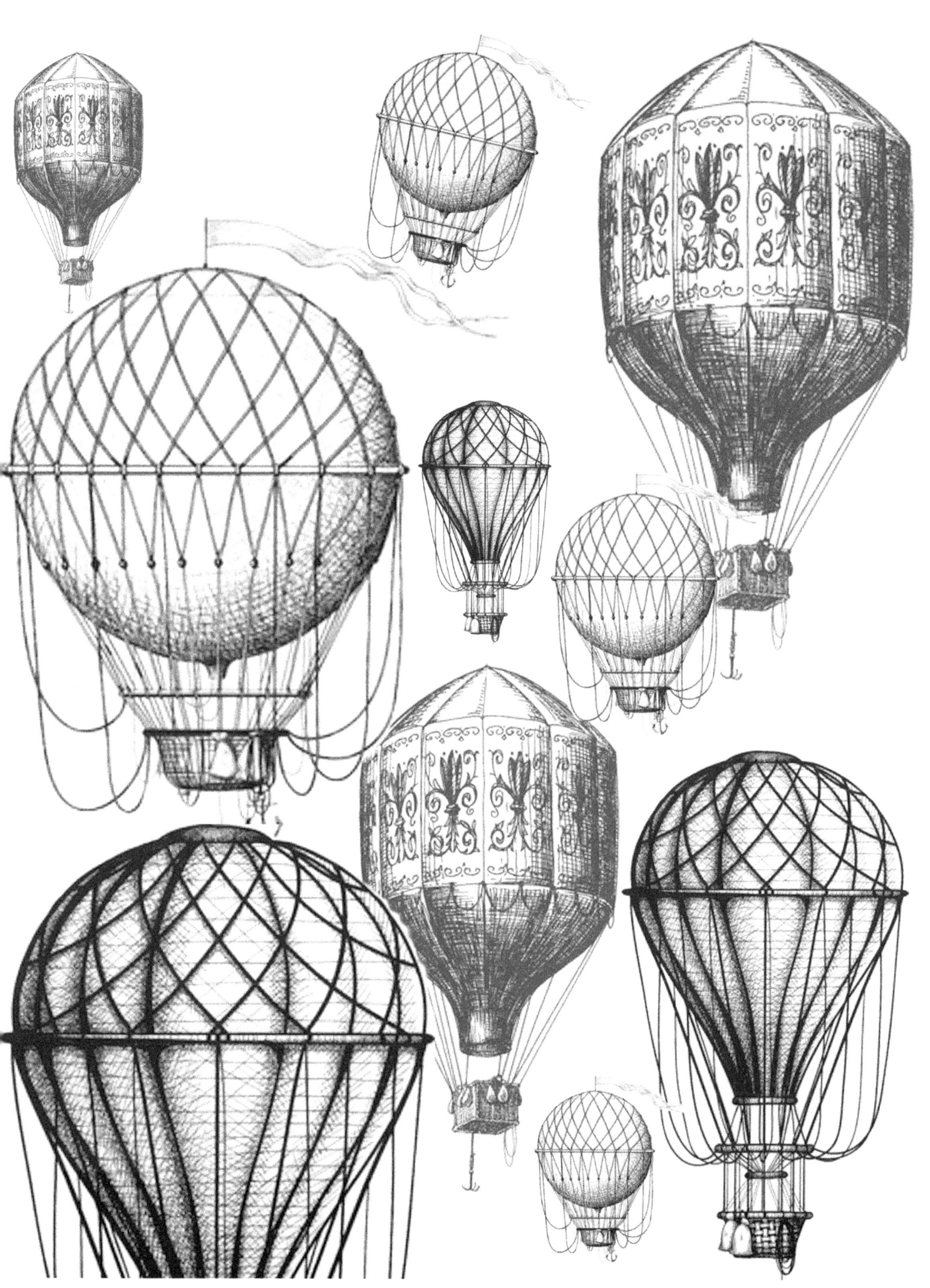

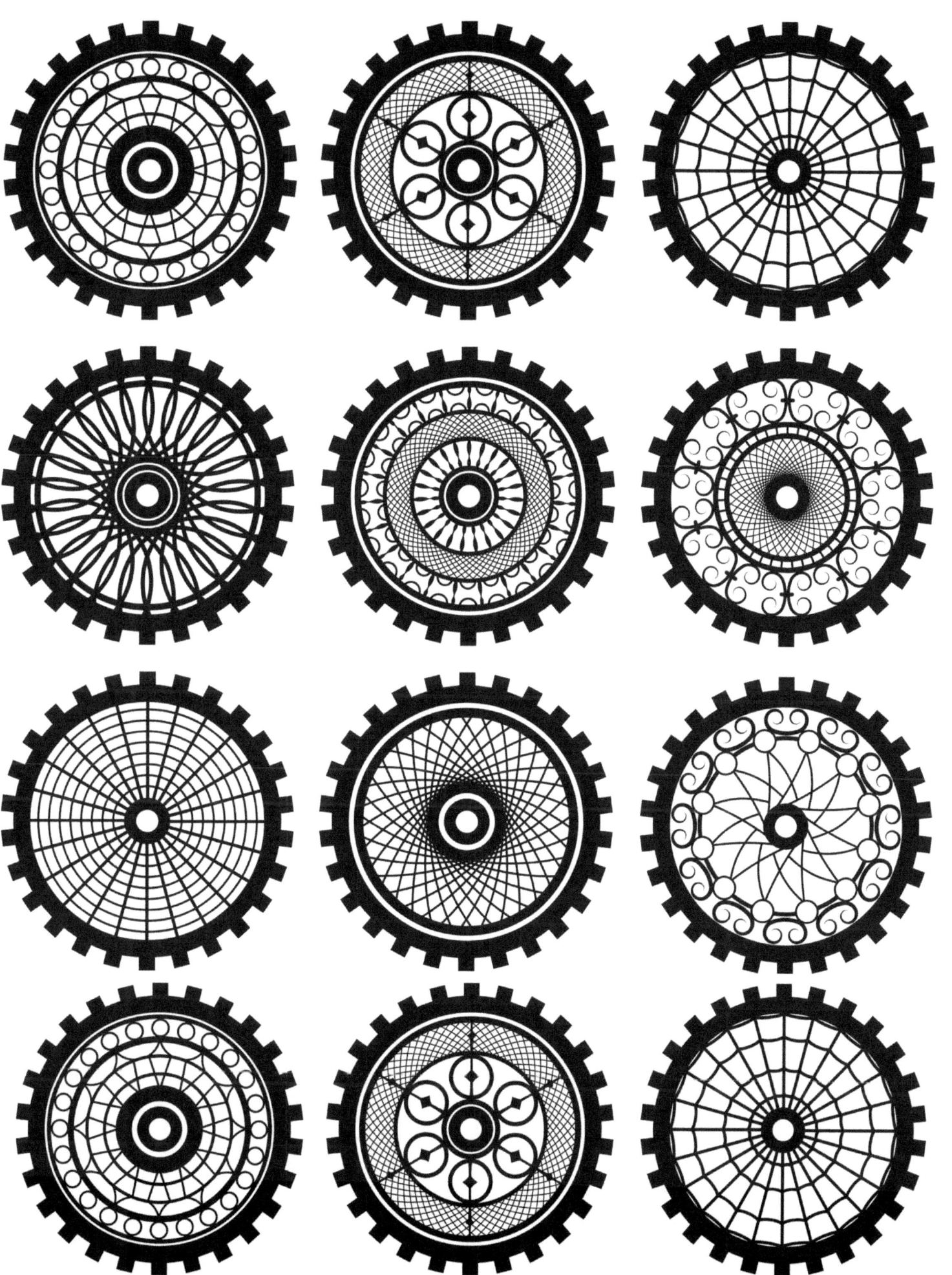

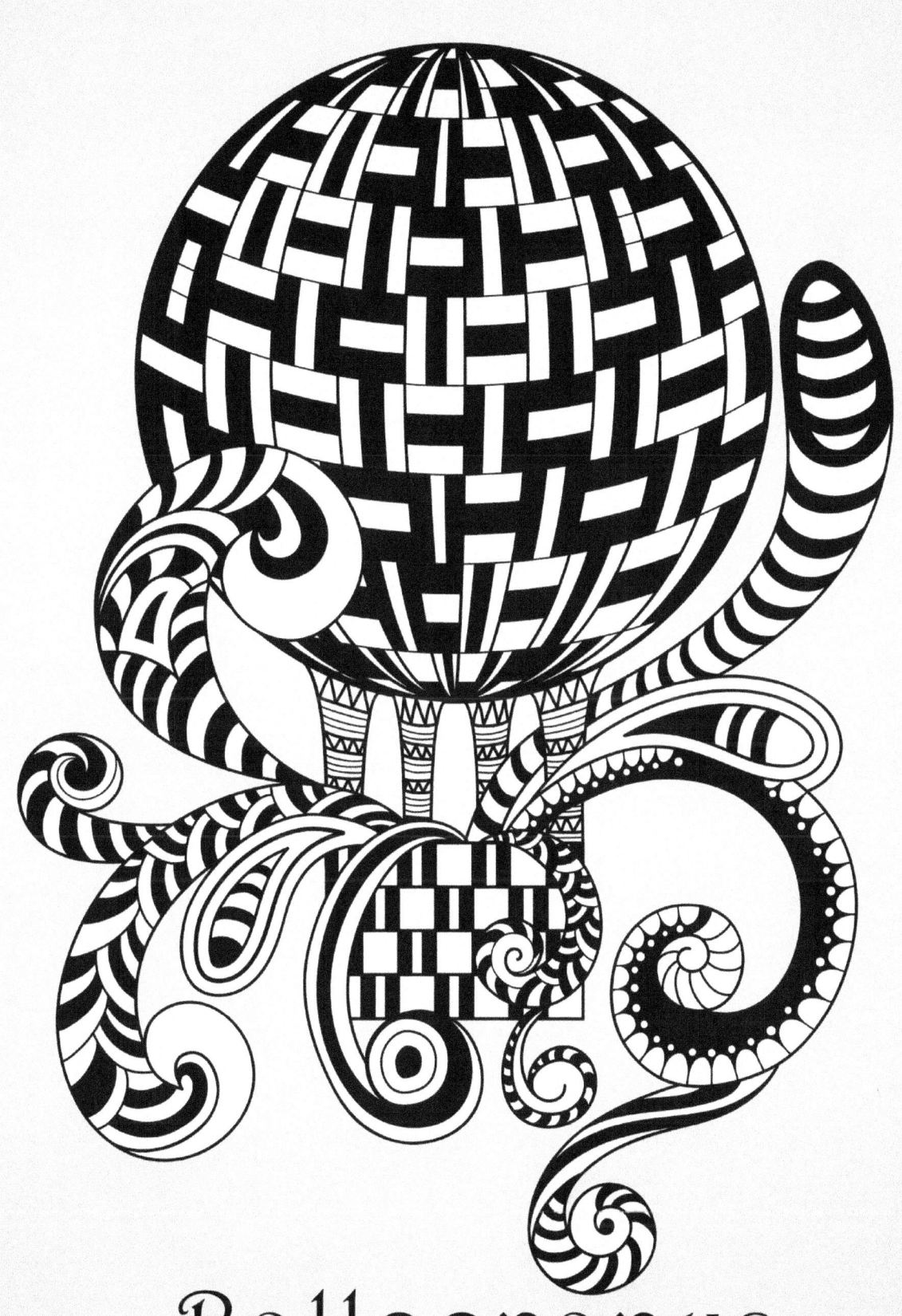

Balloonapus

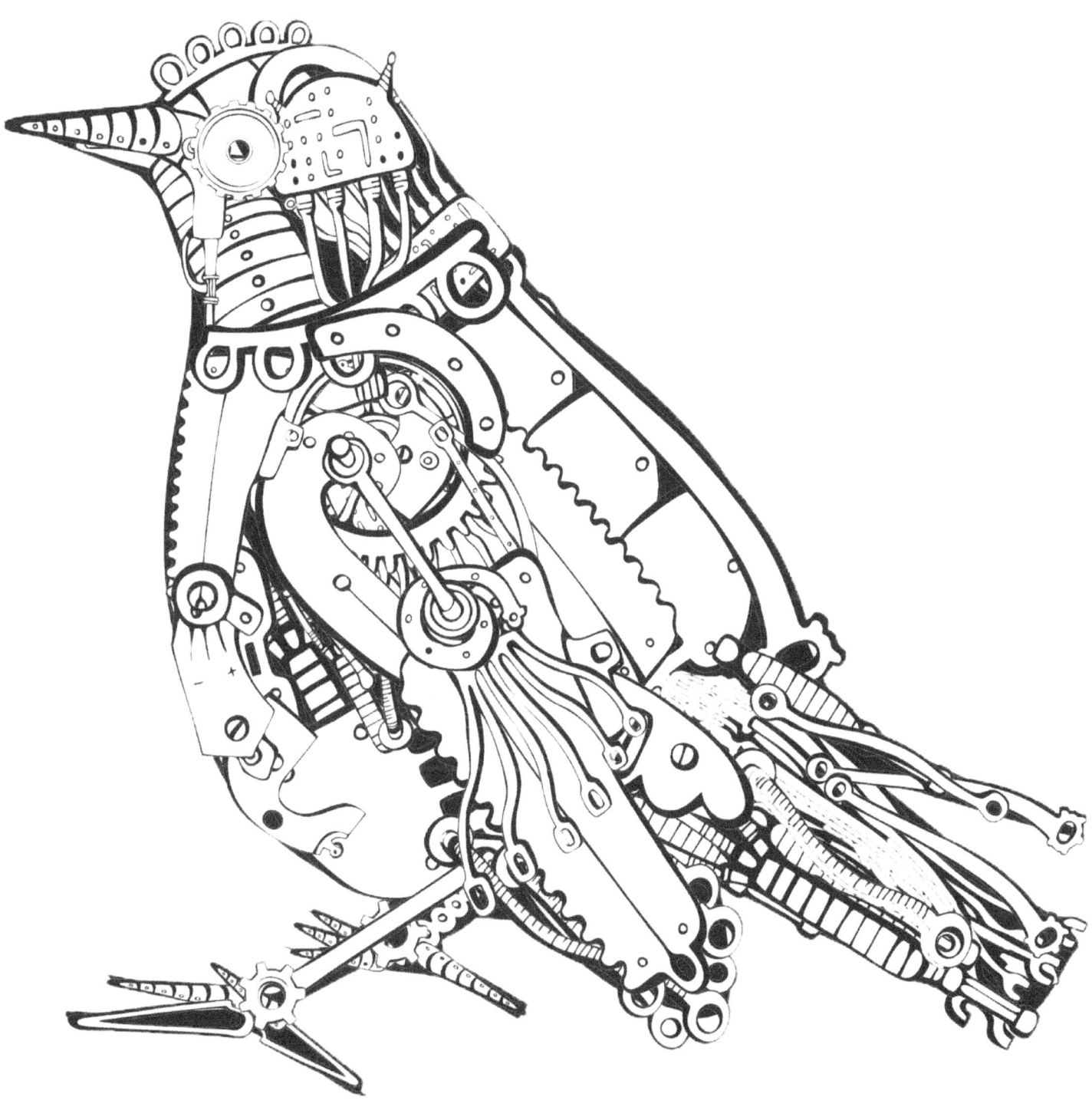

Now that looks fairly simple to operate....hmm, maybe not...

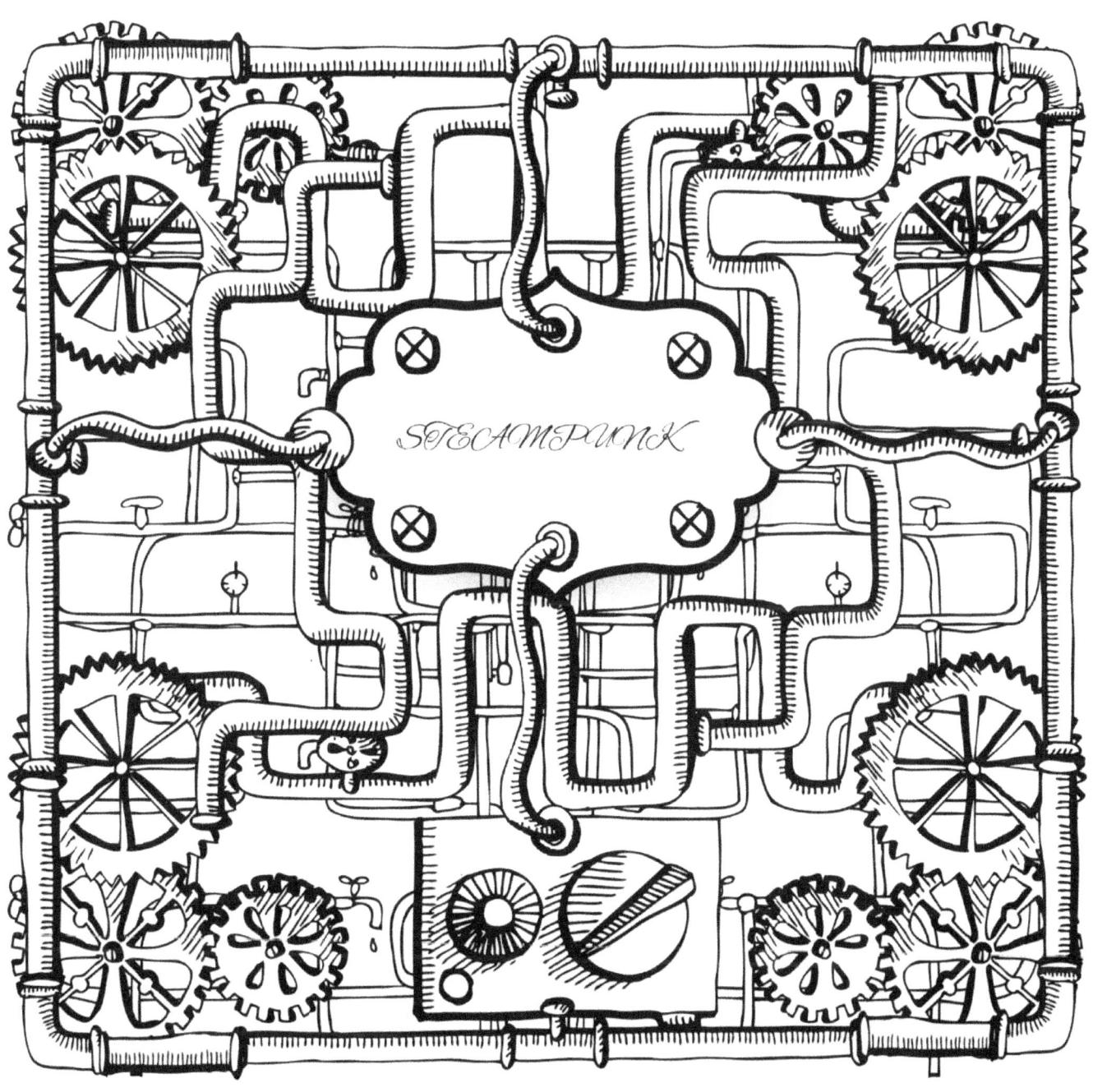

Tophats and goggles, oh my!

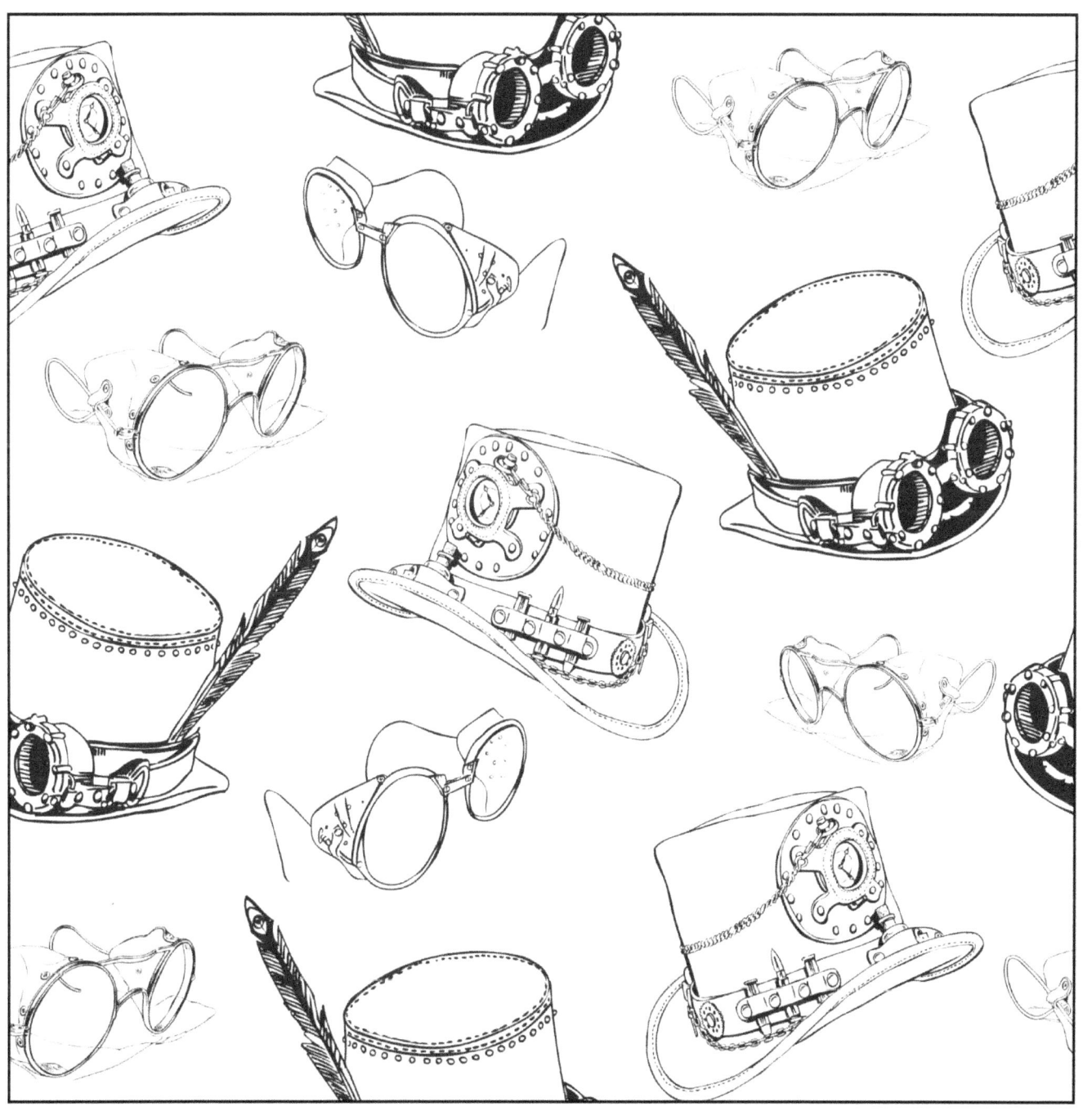

Yikes! Don't press the wrong button!

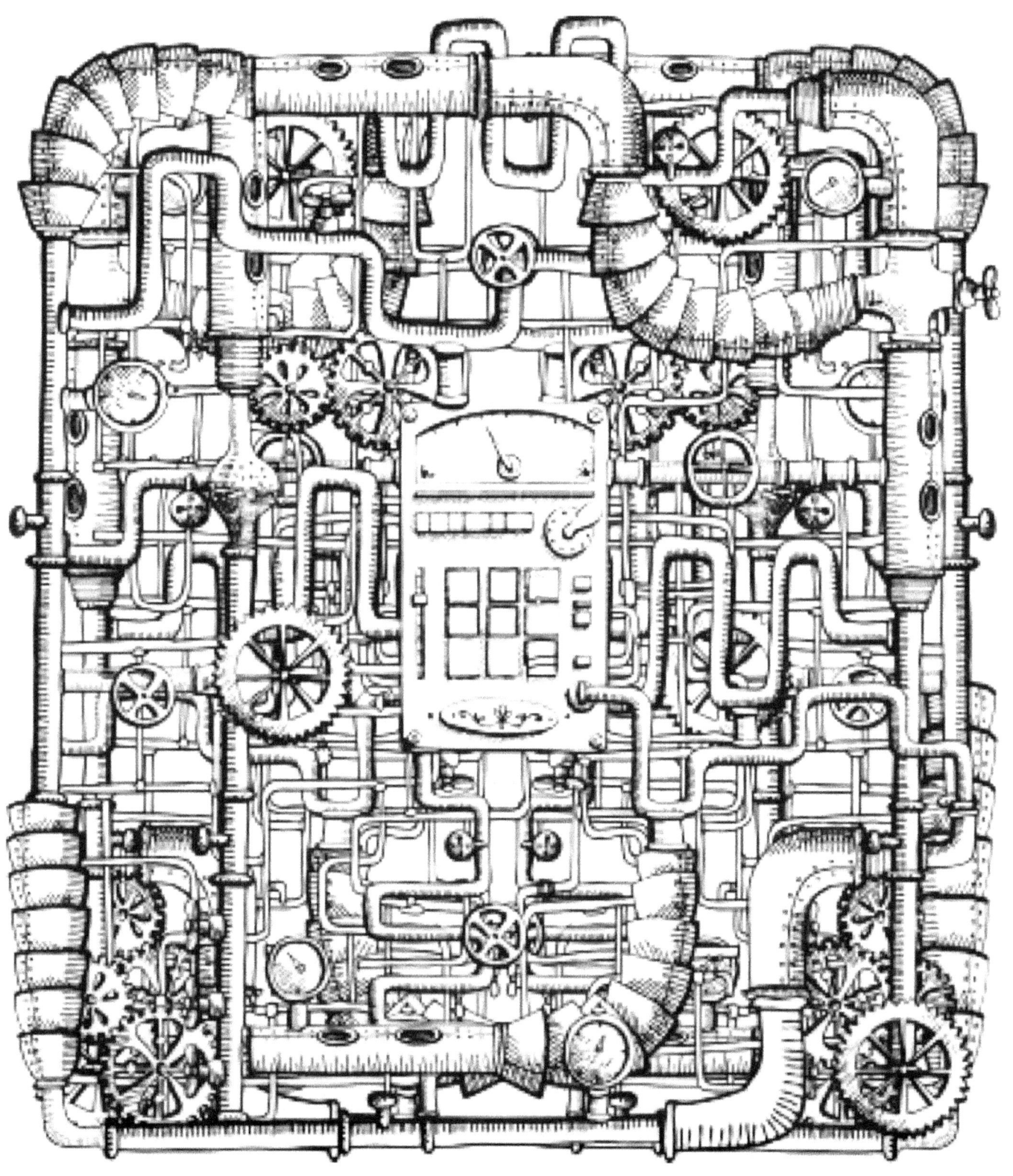

Ok, not totally steampunk, but I like this picture. Hope you do, too!

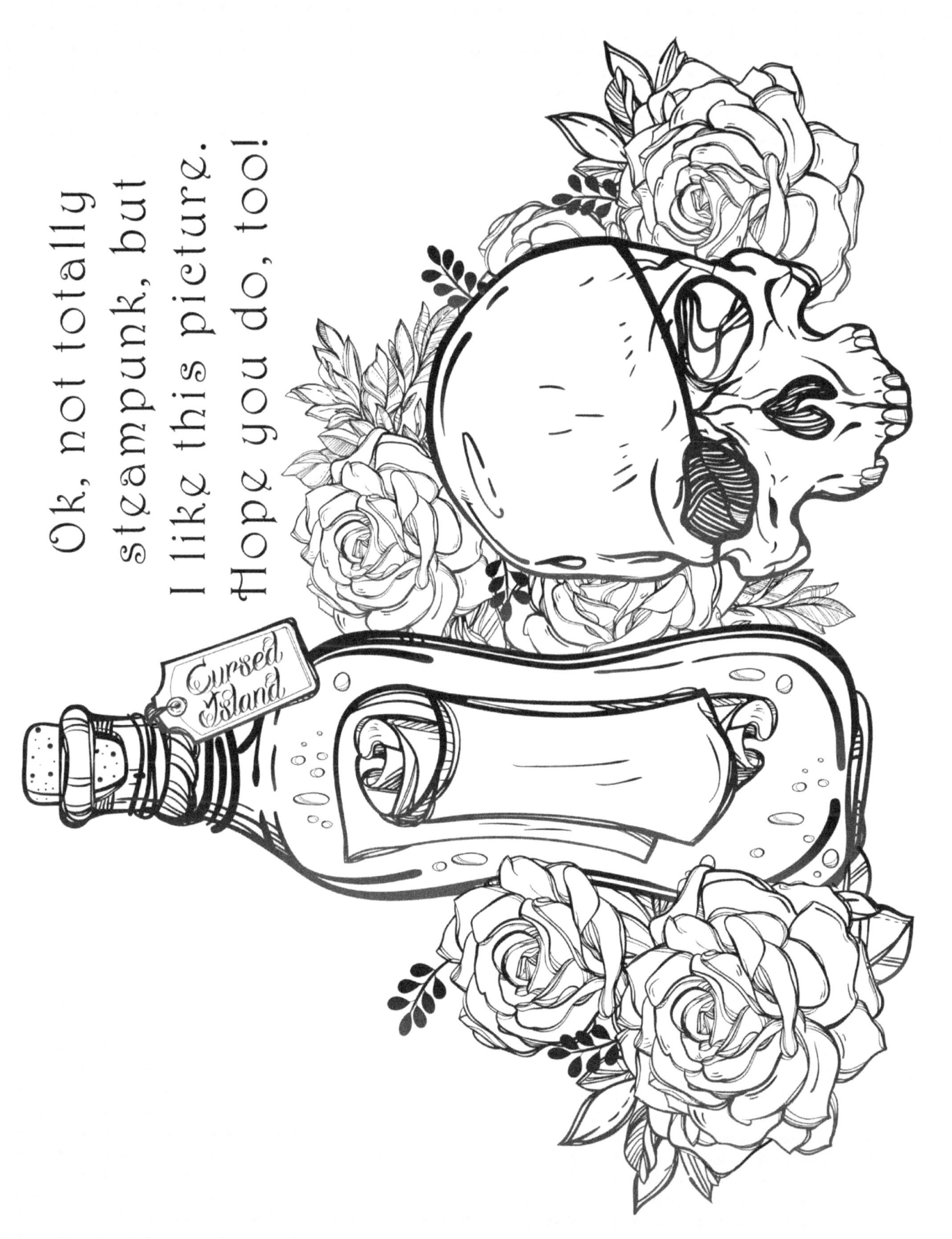

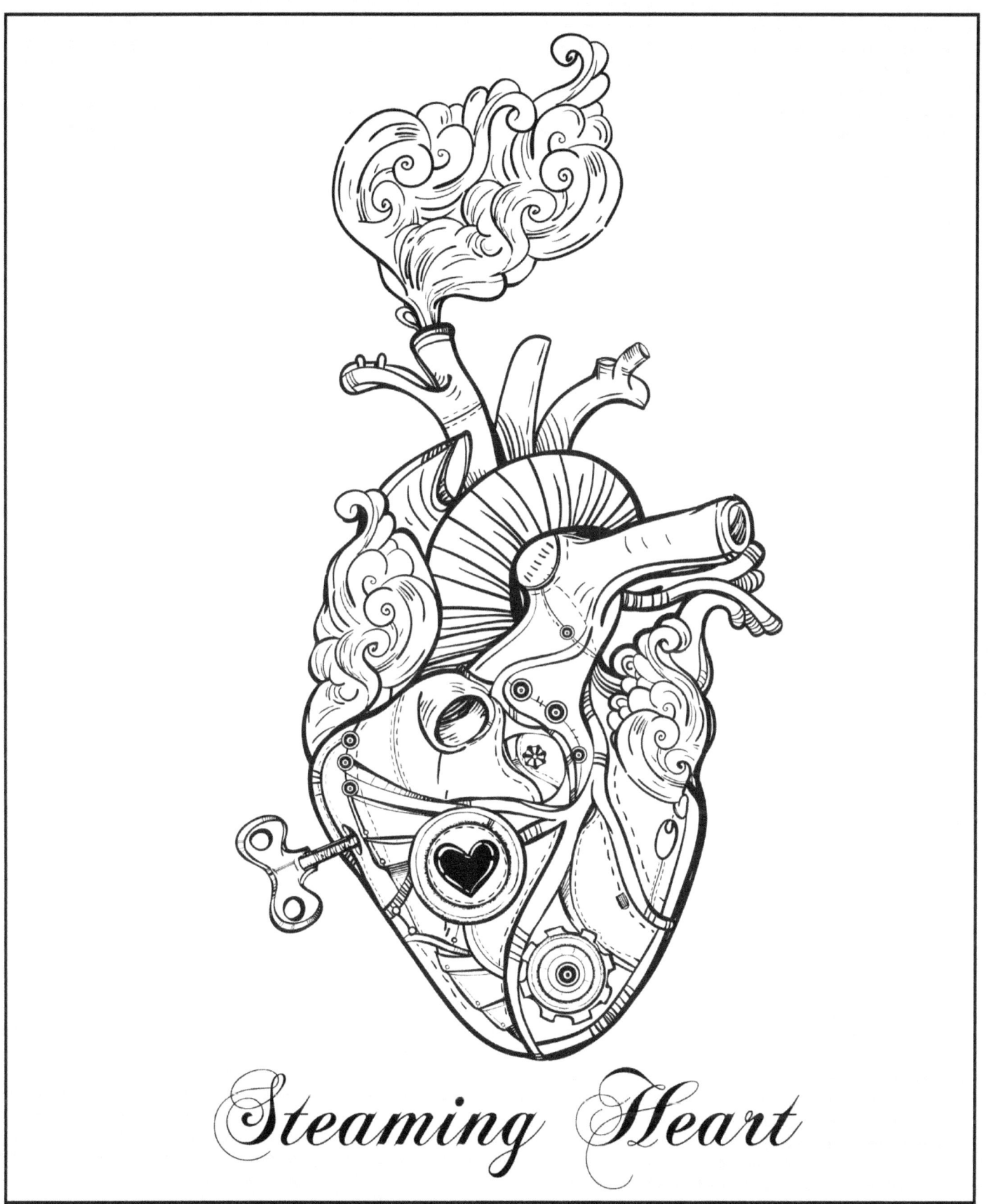

Steaming Heart

Create your own steampunk city...if you don't go blind on this one!

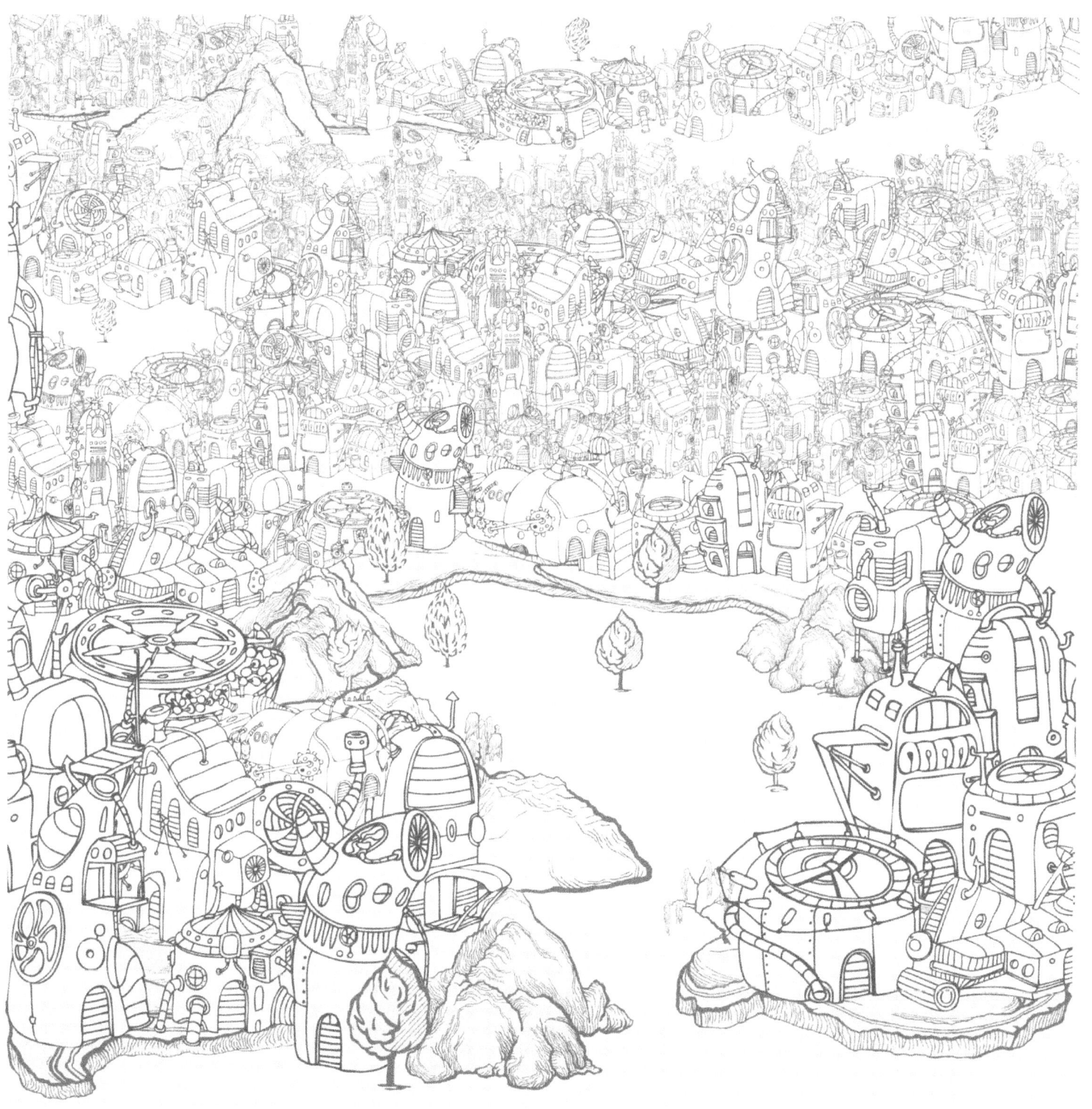

Ah, sweet gear-heart!
Pastels might be pretty here...

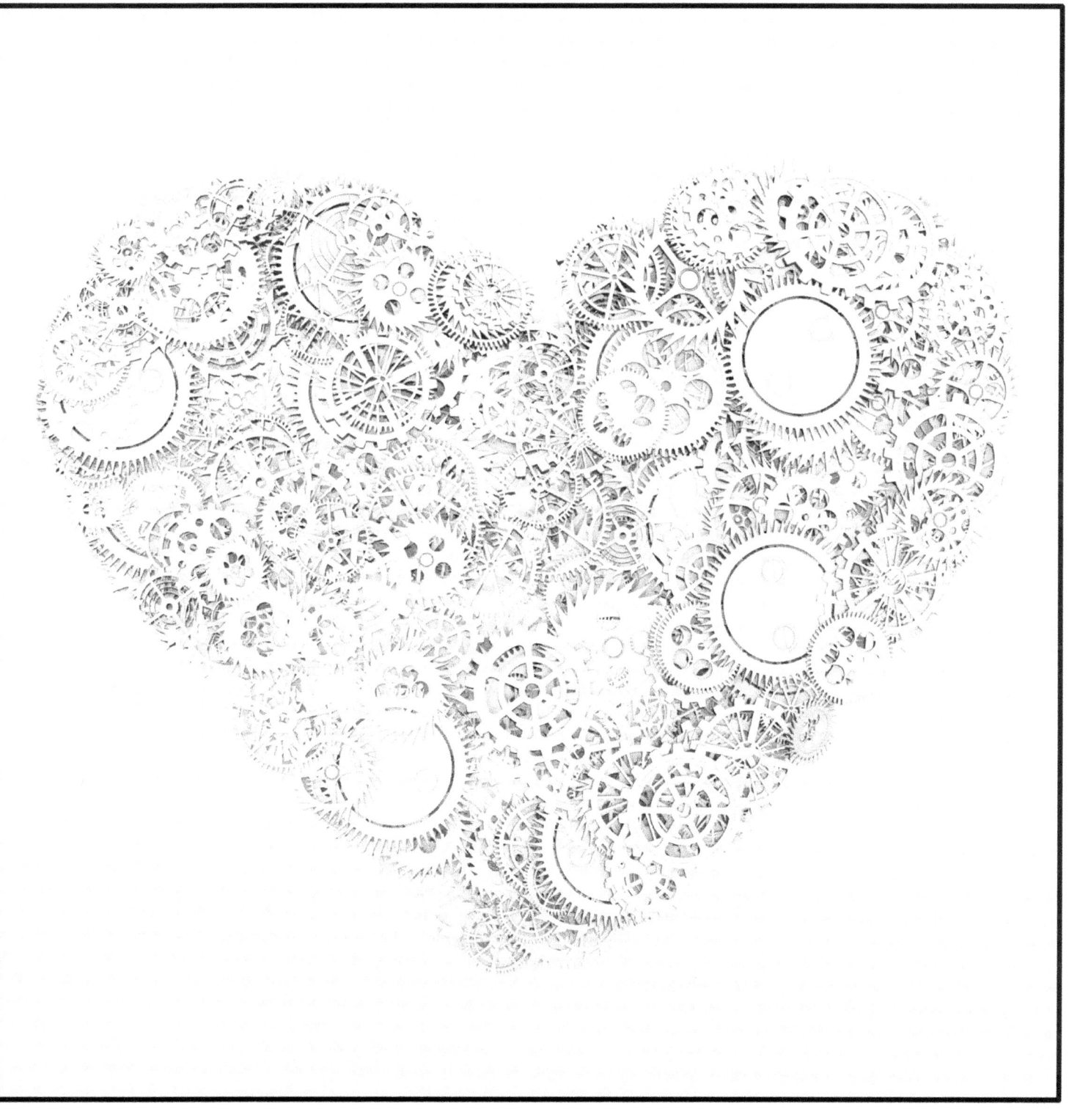

And, a few more gears....

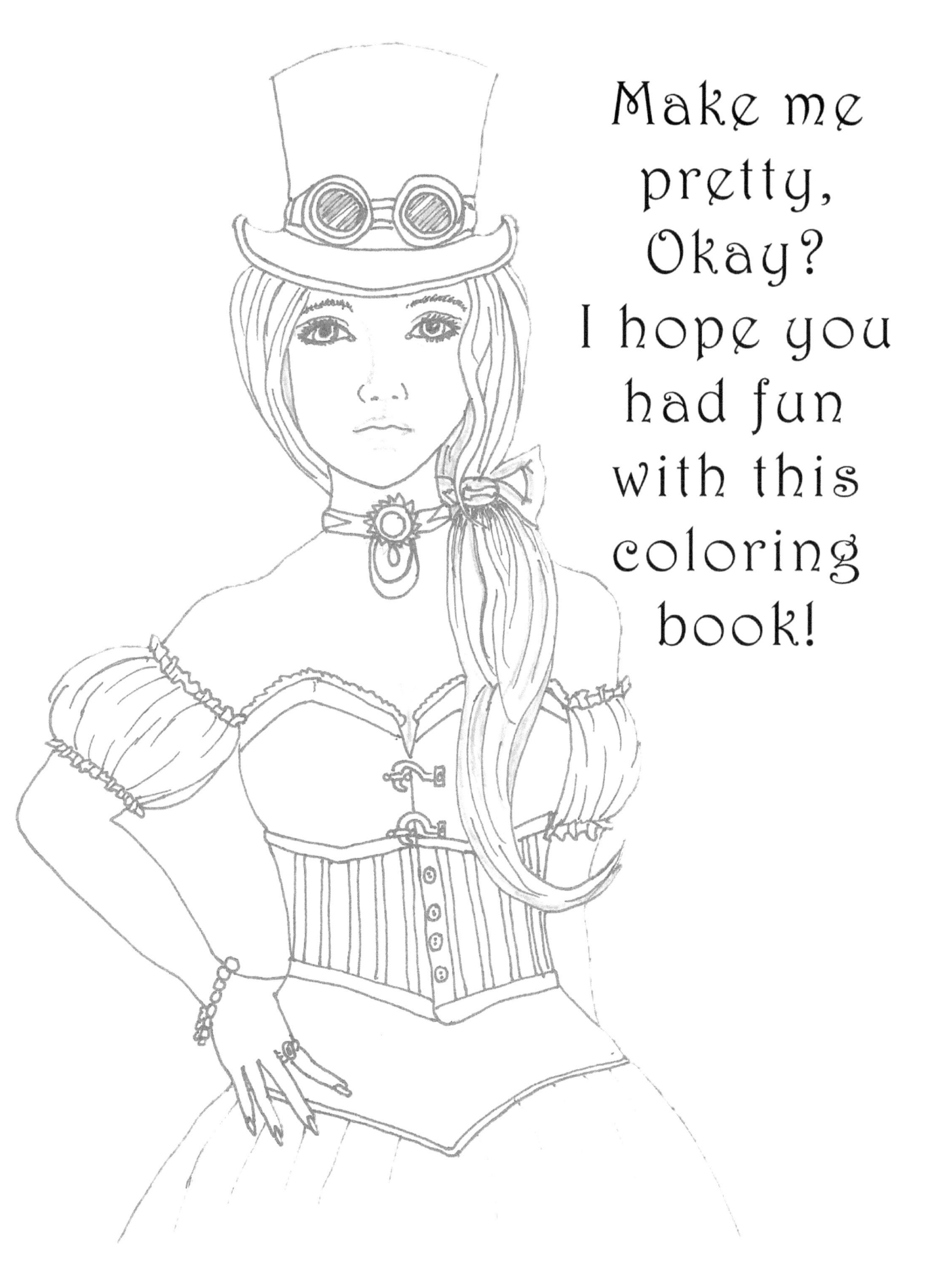

Make me pretty, Okay? I hope you had fun with this coloring book!

I hope you had a great time coloring, and relieved a bit of stress! When you create a masterpiece, go to my Facebook group and post it. Would love to see your work. Ask to join the group and I'll let you in so you can participate. Here's the link: https://www.facebook.com/groups/849091615198919/

If you enjoy steampunk, you might like my novels in the Airship Adventure Chronicles series. They're all available in both electronic and print formats. The first three books are also available as audio books.
Here's a list of the titles:

Airship Adventure Chronicles by Lara Nance

Book one – *Revenge of the Mad Scientist*
Book two – *Rescue from the Baron*
Book Three – *Attack of the Automatons*
Book Four – *Realm of the Ice Queen*
Book Five – *Island at the Top of the World* (coming soon!)

Short story: *The Asylum Prodigy*

For more information on my novels and where to find them, check out my website: www.laranance.com

And have a jolly good day!

www.ingramcontent.com/pod-product-compliance
Lightning Source LLC
Chambersburg PA
CBHW080650180526
45168CB00008B/3371